August Kleinzahler's most recent collection of poems was Red Sauce, Whiskey and Snow. *He is the recipient of numerous awards, including a Guggenheim Fellowship, a Lila Acheson Wallace / Reader's Digest Fund Writer's Award, and an award in literature from the American Academy of Arts and Letters. He lives in San Francisco.*

T0057920

Also by

August Kleinzahler

———

Storm over Hackensack

Earthquake Weather

Like Cities, Like Storms

Red Sauce, Whiskey and Snow

Green Sees Things in Waves

Green Sees Things in Waves

August Kleinzahler

F A R R A R   S T R A U S   G I R O U X

N E W   Y O R K

Farrar, Straus & Giroux
18 West 18th Street, New york, NY 10011

Copyright © 1998 by August Kleinzahler
All rights reserved

Printed in the United States of America
First published in 1998 by Farrar, Straus and Giroux
First paperback edition, 1999

P1

Library of Congress Cataloging-in-Publication Data
Kleinzahler, August.
   Green sees things in waves / August Kleinzahler. — 1st ed.
   p. cm.
   ISBN 0-374-52584-6 (pbk)
   ISBN 978-0-374-52584-2

   I. Title.
PR9199.3.K482G74   1998
811'.54—dc21   *97-34843*

ACKNOWLEDGMENTS

Some of these poems previously appeared in Chicago Review,
Epoch, Harvard Review, London Review of Books, Meanjin,
New American Writing, The New Yorker, Partisan Review,
Shearsman, Threepenny Review, and Verse. "The Dead
Canary" appeared in A Parcel of Poems for Ted Hughes.
"Longitude Lane" appeared in the anthology Literary
Charleston: A Lowcountry Reader (Charleston: Wyrick &
Company, 1996). "Someone Named Gutierrez: A Dream. A
Western" was issued as a broadside by the DIA Foundation
for the Arts, New York, 1996. "Tanka-Toys: A Memoir" was
issued as a pamphlet by X-Ray Press, San Francisco, 1997.
"Uttar Pradesh" appeared in Pushcart Prize XXI, 1996.

To Thom Gunn,

in friendship, in this life

Orteschi met a young lady who,

without any possibility of fraud,

exhaled a strong odor of vanilla from

the commissures of her fingers.

Anomalies and Curiosities of Medicine
GEORGE M. GOULD, M.D.
WALTER L. PYLE, M.D.

Green Sees Things in Waves

Green Sees Things in Waves

Green first thing each day sees waves—
the chair, armoire, overhead fixtures, you name it,
waves—which, you might say, things really are,
but Green just lies there awhile breathing
long slow breaths, in and out, through his mouth
like he was maybe seasick, until in an hour or so
the waves simmer down and then the trails and colors
off of things, that all quiets down as well and Green
starts to think of washing up, breakfast even
with everything still moving around, colors, trails,
and sounds, from the street and plumbing next door,
vibrating—of course you might say that's what
sound really is, after all, vibrations—but Green,
he's not thinking physics at this stage, nuh-uh,
our boy's only trying to get himself out of bed,
get a grip, but sometimes, and this is the kicker,
another party, shall we say, is in the room
with Green, and Green knows this other party
and they do *not* get along, which understates it
quite a bit, quite a bit, and Green knows
that this other cat is an hallucination, right,
but these two have a routine that goes way back
and Green starts hollering, throwing stuff
until he's all shook up, whole day gone to hell,
bummer . . .
      Anyhow, the docs are having a look,
see if they can't dream up a cocktail,

but seems our boy ate quite a pile of acid one time,
clinical, wow, enough juice for half a block—
go go go, little Greenie—blew the wiring out
from behind his headlights and now, no matter what,
can't find the knob to turn off the show.

Snow in North Jersey

Snow is falling along the Boulevard
and its little cemeteries hugged by transmission shops
and on the stone bear in the park
and the WWI monument, making a crust
on the soldier with his chin strap and bayonet
It's blowing in from the west
over the low hills and meadowlands
swirling past the giant cracking stills
that flare all night along the Turnpike
It is with a terrible deliberateness
that Mr. Ruiz reaches into his back pocket
and counts out $18 and change for his LOTTO picks
while in the upstairs of a thousand duplexes
with the TV on, cancers tick   tick   tick
and the snow continues to fall and blanket
these crowded rows of frame and brick
with their heartbreaking porches and castellations
and the red '68 Impala on blocks
and Joe he's drinking again and Myra's boy Tommy
in the old days it would have been a disgrace
and Father Keenan's not been having a good winter
and it was nice enough this morning
till noon anyhow with the sun sitting up there like a crown
over a great big dome of mackerel sky
But it's coming down now, all right
falling on the Dixon-Crucible Pencil factory
and on the spur to Bayonne

along the length of the Pulaski Skyway
and on St. Bridget's and the Alibi Saloon
closed now, 'ho dear, I can't remember how long
and lordjesussaveus they're still making babies
and what did you expect from this life
and they're calling for snow tonight and through tomorrow
an inch an hour over 9 Ridge Road and the old courthouse
and along the sluggish, gray Passaic
as it empties itself into Newark Bay
and on Grandpa's store that sells curries now
and St. Peter's almost made it to the semis this year
It's snowing on the canal and railyards, the bus barns and
    trucks
and on all the swells in their big houses along the river bluff
It's snowing on us all
and on a three-story *fix-up* off of Van Vorst Park
a young lawyer couple from Manhattan bought
where for no special reason in back of a closet
a thick, dusty volume from the '30s sits open
with a broken spine and smelling of mildew
to a chapter titled *Social Realism*

The Dog Stoltz

The dog Stoltz pushed his paw pads into my neck,
the warm, beaten leather deep under my chin,
and let slip the one paw to up near my mouth
with all the filth of the many blocks we trod,
together trod, a well-moistened, adenoidal sound,
part sigh and part growl, coming out of him,
transported, he seemed, in a slow-motion delirium
as I tickled his chest and behind his ear
when he just then told me he'd tear out my throat,
looked in my eye and smiled, best as a dog can,
then turned ruminative and spoke once more:
—*I simply have to knock off that essay on Sassoon.*
This would have been Sassoon the war poet, understand.
Dogs cannot write. My mother told me this.
As for his talk, well, I took no special notice.
His love of the war poets was well known.
Stoltz would have been part bull and something else.
Two friends walked by just then, handily as these things go,
and inquired of us sitting down there on the stoop,
not even, a doorway merely, along a busy street,
how went the day and what pursuits was I attending;
but what interested the two of them most
were the tergiversations of the dog Stoltz,
first beast, then scholar, then abject and adored.
(Say, who among us does not care to be undressed?)
He was not really my dog, you see, and of this made note,
but were glad as well at my having a new dog in my life.

It was a busy stretch of pavement, Amsterdam maybe,
or Broadway, or farther down just south of Chelsea.
I can tell you it was the West Side, of that I'm certain,
and it was mild, spring-like, a few drops in the air.
The friends passed along and the dog Stoltz slept.
He was not my dog, you know. He simply followed me out
of what can only have been a very fine home,
such were his graces, his recondite tastes.
But he was a killer, too, and rather smelled.
I cannot accommodate another animal now, please
      understand.
I am between places. I will yearn for Stoltz, but no.

Watching Young Couples

with an Old Girlfriend

on Sunday Morning

How mild these young men seem to me now
with their baggy shorts and clouds of musk,
as if younger brothers of the women they escort
in tight black leather, bangs and tattoos,
cute little toughies, so Louise Brooks annealed

in MTV, headed off for huevos rancheros
and the Sunday *Times* at some chic, crowded dive.
I don't recall it at all this way, do you?
How sweetly complected and confident they look,
their faces unclouded by the rages

and abandoned, tearful couplings of the night before,
the drunkenness, beast savor and remorse.
Or do I recoil from their youthfulness and health?
Oh, not recoil, just fail to see ourselves.
And yet, this tenderness between us that remains

was mortared first with a darkness that got loose, a frenzy,
we still, we still refuse to name.

Listening in April: Time Zones

(Sydney, Virginia, San Francisco)

I

Rain streams from the stucco parapets
    of the Boomerang Academy
well after midnight, early autumn,
        along this deserted stretch of Broadway
between the railyard and boarded-up Emporium
        where Aunt Peg got her trousseau,
Dolores too, in the year-aught-something
    at the *bottom-of-the-world.*

And it roars in the canopy of leaves
    high above the sedate brick
offices of the law and publishing firms nearby,
        pouring from roof gutters
down on the walkways and out to the street,
    empty of cars but for one.

Inside, Mr. and Mrs. Simão of the cleaning service
    wipe off the waxy leaves
of the potted Monstera, vacuum and dust
    before going back downstairs
to do the toilets and mop. The noise of the machine
    mixes around in or obliterates
the thin plaintive guitar and *fado*
    of the lover who will never return from sea
which comes out of the small yellow tape-player
    sitting there on the floor.

II

And in the glory of Virginia's Piedmont,
     songbirds in full throat
outside the cafeteria of a small, not
     uncharming liberal arts college,
the school dietitian sits weeping
     after lunch in the back
among the stacked steam trays, the fading
     aromas of creamed chipped beef,
carrots and peas, the clatter of silverware.
     She's too proud, he's weak—
or is it the other way round? no matter.
     Azaleas, dogwood—the insult
of their timing, color, fecundity.
     And now the damn peepers starting in, to boot,
with their wall of noise from the lake nearby,
     the pitiless chorus her sobs dig into
like some low coughing horn—
                  fifty, fifty, fifty.

I have for several years now,
      while sitting here in the tub,
fastened onto how the chattering
      of finches and robins,
the hammering, drills and catfights outside,
      the shouts, the trucks double-clutching
(now, this instant, midmorning, San Francisco)
      make rough counterpoint
or interlace with the tune playing
      on the stereo or in my head:

moments, half and quarter moments,
ambushed;
      accident and artifice
so kindred, so swift and unexampled,
      as never to be caught or remembered.

Silver Gelatin

He was watching, looking down at the park
from the 14th floor, waiting.
There is an hour, an afternoon light
well along into winter.

The angle she made with the pram
as she moved past the fountain
could not possibly be improved upon.
Her black hat,

the fur collar and padded shoulders—
a solitary young domestic,
caught through a net of griseous branches,
is getting the baby home for dinner,

home long before dark.
It is terribly cold.
She leans forward, pushing in haste.
At her own now extreme angle

and with the black coat and hat,
the pram underneath her,
the snow underfoot,
she looks, for all the world, from here,

a broken-off piece of Chinese ideogram
moving across the page.

Uttar Pradesh

You were dozing over Uttar Pradesh
well after the shadows of Annapurna
swept across the big plane's starboard wing,

dreaming a peevish little dream
of Stinky Phil, your playground tormentor
from fifty years before, his red earmuffs

and curious cigar voice vivid as the tapioca
you used to gag on at the end of Thursday lunch,
when the captain's serene, patriarchal voice

suggested you buckle up, moments before
the plane jumped then yawed in an air pocket
and dropped five hundred feet. Oh shit,

there goes the Parcheesi board and what's left
of a very bold Shiraz. Melissa
purses her lips in the compact mirror,

turns a quarter left, then right a tad,
scowls at her mascara and snaps it shut with a sigh.
You are the preeminent colorist

of your era. Some would suggest a fraud
with your grand chevelure of white hair and cape.
Mother would certainly not disagree,

but here you are again, crossing continents,
six miles above the petty quarrels,
the tossed green salads and car wrecks

to receive yet another prize, a ribbon,
a princely sum in a foreign capital
and a spread on the Sunday culture page.

How very far away now seem your student days:
happy, hungry, cooking up manifestos,
turpentine, pussy, stale cigarette smoke.

It was evident from the start. It screamed
at you from billboards, fabric shops, museums;
and no one else saw it, no one but you.

Amazing. Then half a lifetime to execute it
in paint. What a long time with one idea.
But still, it was a doozy, put you

in the art books and kept you there for life.
There will be a car waiting when you arrive.
Kremer is visiting with the Philharmonic

and will do the Sibelius, your favorite.
You recall meeting him some years ago
at a dinner in—Cologne, I think it was.

An intense young man, but very pleasant.
Right, now you remember the evening,
the lugubrious molding and burgundy drapes . . .

Ah, yes, and a most memorable *hasenpfeffer*.

Tanka-Toys: A Memoir

The planet may have tilted, if only a hint
when the shelf of cloud burnt angrily
before dusk
         jack-o'-lantern stuff

her hair the color of her coat,
fall wear

———

The wet stain her bathing suit left
on the bench
         the shape of Bolivia,
drying, drying into atolls
Ursa Minor, a thumbprint

———

It was at Herbie's place, no
Pinckney's, she showed us her pubes
and long shadow of thigh

The fresh linen smelled so sunnily like
What did the lady on TV call it?

An orchard of some kind

Sure it's just like staring
out the window, Johnny
sure

but with fly eyes
and sidewise

———

When Pappy and Mahoney left
for dinner and a show

I was soooo a-LONE
there in the doorway, sore way
of being the phone ringing

It was summer again and green

———

You do turkey, baby, I like peas
snap beans, oyster sauce, fuzzy

blond roux

―――

The clues to my being—
the bloody windsprint

the mashie niblick hanging
from a willow

the retreating aria

―――

The way the *spaldeen* jumped left
instead of right

and died on your square of sidewalk
that Friday afternoon so long ago

That's all you need to know

―――

Oh, I was freed
freed, I say

kneeling, teething

chopchopchopping
like a tractor piston

like an outboard coughing up lake

A Sketch of Gael Turnbull

on a Visit from Edinburgh

It's in the manner your head turned,
just perceptibly,
when the little man, who had been inching closer,
furtively,
for several minutes at least,
began to speak.

No surprise at his curious aspect,
the wee tiny child-man
with thick glasses, wisp of goatee, belly,
whom I've seen for years
cheerfully fuddled outside the corner market
with never even a *by-your-leave*

when I greeted him in passing.
No surprise or difficulty with the muddy speech
in a foreign English
as the two of you discussed the view
from the heights there,
sweeping across sea, park and downtown,

the Marin hills beyond
and a big tanker vanishing over the horizon.
In great earnest
trading impressions, you nodding

gravely as an official of state.
You both looked about the same age, owlish and 60.

And something in your posture as well,
erect, slightly magisterial,
the minister's boy, gentle but severe,
as the simple man came slowly to a boil,
bit by bit leaning ever further
into the lee of you.

Vulture Under the Palisades

The park road is closed in winter

But they let you through on foot

The mile or two to the base of the cliffs

The vast stretch of river

Through bare growth

And apartment blocks on the far shore

Catching the pink light of late afternoon

Along their crests. Very still

Occasional birdsong and the distant rush

Of snowmelt from the culverts built into basalt

What they once called *bluestone* hereabouts

Until you round the bend

And there's the bridge

Rising 600 feet from its pier in the shallows

You pass underneath

And the low roar and thrumming of traffic

Swallows everything else around it

Until there is no you

But then you pass through, back into the silence

The sough of water from the Palisades

And you smell the river and tidal flats

That's when you spot it

Perched high in the branches at the water's edge

What you at first mistake for a raven

Dangling something from its beak

When it turns to look down at you

With that narrow russet instrument of face

Then back to the river and spreads its wings

On First Looking into

Joseph Cornell's Diaries

The sopressata fée outside of Calfasso's
with the swept-back 'do and blood on her smock
grabs a quick smoke on the sidewalk,
tosses it in the gutter then sucks back her lips
till they smack, getting her lipstick right.
                              Fierce little thing . . .
My freight elevator makes a distant whump
then squeals to a stop on one of the floors back there
behind my left ventricle.
                    OUT OF SERVICE
for months, I am at first alarmed then refreshed.

————

What a preposterously spring-like day on Anderson Avenue
for the depths of February.
                    You can hear the snow melt
under the parked cars, and the #4 School crossing guard,
burly and mustachioed, reminds me just then
of an elderly Victor McLaglen, a favorite of the children
and somewhat stooped in his waning years
but ever that loyal and gallant pal from *Gunga Din.*

————

Try as I might now for weeks I still cannot find
the space I need to contain the Clorox label
which would go behind and to the right
of the orange box of gelatin stool softeners.

———

There is that and the far larger dilemma,
one that has resisted me and my wiles for years:
to find a distillate or tincture
of daytime TV commercials for the ladies—
Pond's cold cream, say, or diaper rash powders—
then somehow reconstitute and *fashion the flavor*
to a doctor's waiting room and a blue plastic chair
(in the modern Italian design style)
with a splayed, greasy *Mademoiselle*
from the previous June left underneath.

(Oh, but if I could only unknot that one
every arroyo and vista would open up to me)

I go park awhile outside the boarded-up Dairy Queen
and try to find Fauré's *Berceuse.*
                              A gust of wind
rocks the car, just perceptibly,
and then it comes to me, is served up to me, really:

warm butterscotch syrup and the Little League parade.

———

My *condition* intrudes
and all the air goes right out of me.
It is the bad feeling. I call it *Dolph.*
It smells of roofing tar and makes my pineal gland itch,
itch till it aches.

It spreads into my extremities and lays waste my strength
so that never again will my inventions come to life:

that little green chutney bottle in a field of stars
and the doll's taffeta apron . . .

nor will I bathe ever again with the divine Mavlakapova
in my special Thursday dream.

Gray Light in May

The soft gray light between rains
This enveloping light
Under a canopy of green
Oak   chestnut   maple
Last night the moon, orange and full
Over Manhattan's West Side
Edgewater below so sleepy
The neighborhood asleep
My family asleep
Coming back here how many years now
And the ride in from Newark
Manhattan looming over the meadows
The beauties of travel are due to
The strange hours we keep to see them
This soft windless air
Away now nearly thirty years
You can smell the tidal flats below
Passenger jets silent overhead
In and out of Kennedy, La Guardia
As if gliding across the night
My heart abrim
A glass of wine, spilling over
The air like wine
I am a stranger to myself

The soft gray light
The still moist air

The azaleas in these yards
Under the canopies of leaves
Fiercely abloom in this gray light
Between rains
Almost stereoscopic
The broad green leaves overhead as well
Painters know it, photographers too
The smell of lilac
Nudging my chest like the muzzle of a dog
The manner in which this gray light
Wraps itself around things
Saturating them
Bringing up their color
So much a part of me
So much of what is dearest
I can barely stand upright under the weight of it
The song of the wood thrush
Reverberates through the heavy air
And around its hidden columns
Who knows the Palisades as I do
Lilac and dogwood
Flowering pear blossoms, mingling
Drifting in gutters
How many years
For how many years
A stranger to my own heart

Glossolalia All the Way to Buffalo

Poppy is in the storm cellar, cleaning.
Chippie and her little friend Arlene
up top are riding along on the swells
of a joke about the Russian tank commander,
Colonel Vladimir Khotchokakov.
They are beside themselves, each wave
of laughter gaining force from the one before
until their faces redden for want of breath.

Their laughter is to Poppy as water
falling from a jagged height in broad curtains
to the rocks below. The violent
little spasms, hiccups, retching nearly,
moves the feel from the grotto or bosky glen
to the clangorous, windswept gorge.

—*How like an intoxicant,* thought Poppy
to himself, the way words come loose
of their moorings and fall apart,
little bits of them all over like an airliner wreck
spread out across the phrenologist's chart,

as he pushed aside a cobweb, wall-sized,
something really from the Brothers Grimm,
and found there only a rusted nozzle
and the mummy of, well, a *largish* mouse.

As if the bus at day's end from the plant
back to the suburb turned right
on Marsh Tern Road instead of the straight shot
south to the agapanthus and satellite dish
then made a hard left to the finca near La Paz.

The laughter, sobs and coughs subside.
—*My darling, my little baby girl,* Poppy sighs,
the notion a cool, sunwashed breeze
across the back of his neck, now starting
to simmer with an itch, maybe prickly heat,

when he just then remembers a line
spoken or read in a recent dream, the words
so charged as to be an incantation or charm,
transforming the landscape to nothing but light—
no chairs, no stovepipe, no glue,

nothing but those words, stenciled in air,
sky-written across a creamy expanse,
spoken and written as one:
                              a cipher, a code, but drab,
weirdly so, like the password of a fraternal order
with its special hats and showcase full of civic honors:

He used to own a bar in Buffalo.

West

An apocalyptic crack spreads like thunder
over sintered gorges and alkali flats.
The junco is knocked sideways then drops
as if shot onto a granite bed, turning
slowly mahogany there—wild peony.
Somewhere in the bleached sky and cirrus a Phantom
is at play, singeing cattle, lifting shingles
off farmhouse roofs. An enormous ball
of phosphorus bounds across the Carson Sink.

—Christ, it was hot out there on Jackass Flats
after that big wave of wire, sagebrush
and rattlesnakes broke over us.

The Paiute flint auger fairly hummed
with chromium when they pulled it out of Stillwater
    Marsh.
You could listen to it like a conch shell,
an impossibly busy, serial music
that compounds and accelerates, on and on.

Longitude Lane

The oleander on Longitude Lane
flares among the languors and fevers of June
below the south-facing piazzas
the sea breezes find
or don't quite find
along the corridors of ivy-covered brick
Carolina *gray brick* and wrought iron
that wind away inland from the Battery

History just sits out there, a kind of weather
in the harbor and beyond
on the plantations and through the low country
with its bogs and herons
its skirmishes never forgotten

And the manners in town so antique, so elegant
an underwater Kabuki in summer dresses
The old families and Huguenot names

The long siege and storied cannonades

Turkey buzzards over the market
water rats under the pantry

The precious settee and the wild, wild daughters

September: Johnson County, Iowa

The hills press down
with their brawn and queer angles,
the soybeans reddish brown,
corn a week or two from silage.
If you didn't already know
the famous white house
was just down the road
you'd still guess where you were
from the paintings—
                    Spring Turning
Death on the Ridge Road
    Haying   Near Sundown

Friends of many years,
two old ladies, both raised
on the land, gone to the city:
large lives,
given, got, lost or forgotten,
back home where they started,
alone now,
at ease on the long verandah.

The one chewing parsley
picked fresh from the pot,
the other, mock-stern,
taking it all in:

—Oh, go right ahead,
if you don't the grasshoppers will.

Rain in the south. Wind picking up.
The crumbling house of another century,
damp in the two-foot-thick brick walls.
Big rigs in the far distance.
The little old lady from Dubuque—
still slender with the model's cheekbones
but the teeth gone brown
and higgledy-piggledy.

A grocery bag in front of her
the friend brought from town
full of magazines and the *Sunday Times*
she'll read by the fire all winter.
And out come the beautiful old manners:
—Oh, what, whatever in the world,
might they be up to, do you suppose,
in New York, these days?
                            Some food in there
as well, some cookies,
and tucked way down deep
a bottle of wine.

The first drops begin to fall.
Tractors outside sprawling frame homes.

—You can grow anything in this soil,
anything at all.
                   A few cattle grazing
in a swale off the road.
Very still. The rain coming on now.
—The callow ones,
the ones who didn't like the work,
simply kept on heading west.

The Flock of Blackbirds

The flock of blackbirds in advance of the storm
folds and unfolds as one,
changing planes across the wind
the way parallelograms move
across computer screens, cooling the points
as they turn through themselves
driven by an algorithm
into new shapes that bend and dissolve
only to reappear and move on
to the next set of coordinates,
on and on toward some helical destiny

beyond conjuring as I chewed my yucca
and watched them with a friend
loop and slide over the parking lot
across the street and drift
backward over a stand of tulip trees
as if at play, hovering.
It had been a wet spring
and the radio was calling for another two inches.

Was it that weekend or the next—
I forget—
            but it was late, too late
for the train back,
her pupils big as grapes, when out they came,
just like that,   1   2   3

dropped as if calving:

                      "esclavizar"

   "negrier"

        "schmarotzer"

Tiered, undulant rows of pins dropped
precisely into place,
and I felt it, I swear,
at the bottom of my diaphragm,
a tiny rush of displaced air.

They Ofttimes Choose

They ofttimes choose to pause naked at the door
if in the morning they are well pleased,
then turn with a flourish back to their toilette.

I have more than the one time beheld,
whether Corinna, Meg or Philomel,
that grand, nay, regal posture till my gaze

was snared in hers and tenderly led down,
that I might see, might know one moment more
the abundance there flesh can barely contain—

oh, the freshets, the unaccountable dolors—
then she, with one long last ferocious look,
would burn me deep yet leave no wound or pain.

II

Then take their leave but are not truly gone,
for amidst the cushions and disarray
bracelets and earrings, a kerchief I'll find.

They, who are not careless in other ways,
are careless neither in what they leave behind
as well as where. For when I spy it there

half-hidden in a fold or by an emptied glass
they are already several hours passed
from my mind as well as last embrace

but return now in full if not in flesh.
How well these ladies do contrive, how well,
to keep me in thrall with their sweet neglect.

For Ann,

Whose Studio Burnt to the Ground

in the Big Futon Factory Fire Across

the Freeway from the Coliseum

A cinder in the left fielder's eye, then a tear.
It has been a bad swing west for the Yanks,
ten behind the Sox coming in and, looks like,
about to fall another game back tonight.

In the shadows, between the bleachers
and banks of floodlights high overhead
on their stanchions, the radiance visible for miles
from the freeway and hills, through the windows

of planes as they dip, heading in and out,
is an atmosphere, or strip of atmosphere,
a kind of sedimentary layer
of smoke and ash from ten thousand futons,

plaster and industrial carpets, the bonsai
next to the warehouse elevator
along with your ellipsoids on canvas,
arranged this way and that, rutabagas

hard by summer squash, brushing up against
buttocks and yams—*sexual tubers,*

I liked to call them and so did you.
How nice to register the world in shapes

you might squeeze or eat. Better than words,
plus you can get your hands dirty, like work,
but fun, like playing in the grass at night,
pounding your mitt and thinking of yams.

That big kid will be washed up in five years,
coaching Pony League in Saranac Lake,
and you, my friend, will be on to your next thing,
a fresh vein, spaghetti creatures, papier-mâché.

Think, this summer forty years ago on 52nd Street
Lennie Tristano's quartet was in the Sing Song Room
of the Confucius Restaurant, playing "Mean to Me."
They've played it every night for weeks,

but tonight, when Konitz finishes his solo
and Lennie digs back in, just then,
the hair stands up on everyone's neck
while the bass feeds him lines he tears into bits.

The tape machine is on the blink that set,
and those two solos, like a million more,
escape through the exhaust fan and into the night,
rising along with the car horns and shrieks

until a breeze takes hold and carries them south
then east over Brooklyn and the lights of Ebbets Field
out to Sheepshead Bay and Rockaway Beach,
swirling awhile then heading off to sea.

Napping After Lunch

(For J.A. on the occasion of his 70th)

On the tea-green comforter with Babette
the pet mouse
stuffed and at sea on its expanse
a breeze in the curtains
how one then begins to float
naked but for fur as God would have
so many towns
unseen at first then bend after bend revealed
the distant slap and creaking of tackle
the great cedar and the fountain's plashing
I recall, don't you
say so, say you do
the bays, the teeming estuaries
say to me how possibility's everywhere welcome

A hint of lavender, from the soap, perhaps the yard
out there with the swells of noise
of crowds on the cobbled quay, seaplanes
trembling in the curtains
the green dial, among the many signals
in there in the other room on the radio glowing
adrift like a dinghy
a mile maybe more away from shore
out there heedless, unmanned
the fading steel guitar

what sounds like Veronica's pattymelt song
then clearly, the wind chimes on Nana's porch
a clap of thunder
and at last long last host upon host of mummers

Sunday Morning

How oddly content, these dogs of the homeless,
asleep at their feet in doorways, under benches,
good, healthy coats, breathing easily

Sunday morning in the fog downtown, in the quiet
as the hotels and neighborhoods awaken
to clouds of eggs and excrement, the chatter

on color TVs, spectacular reds and greens.
The ragged sleepers tremble under blankets
of newsprint, cough, turn over, curl as far

into themselves as they can, careening through
the switchbacks of dreams, fighting the wheel
as they barrel downhill, working that clutch

till the brakes go . . . *Oh*, with a muffled cry,
suddenly in the world like newborn babes,
except on Market, filthy and cold.

The dog opens one eye, no trouble, old routine.
Sighs and dozes off again, snoring
a thin wheezing snore, muzzle to sidewalk.

He is a well-looked-after animal,
fed as best as one can, touched, held.
The man tickles behind his dog's ear.

Fella's ear twitches. He calls him *Fella*.
That's what the guy he got him off called him.
Good, brown, short-haired mutt,

not too dumb and doesn't make a big fuss.
All of his pleasure, all that's left of love—
ridiculous, tragic: 45 lbs. of snoring dog.

But it's mutual, you see, and genuine.
Real as warm food in an empty belly.
And, in fact, that's just what it is for them both:

Fella's dog smell, the heat that raises it,
and that sour, musty smell the man has,
they all have, the stairwells and walls have

wherever they congregate. But Fella's friend
has his very own, very delicious smell,
a bit like old bones, urine, soup.

Monsters

. . . and thus of what she earst had beene
Remayned nothing in the worlde.
OVID, *Metamorphoses*

Lie down then with the monsters
Take your ease
They frightened you once
But not anymore
You awaken among them
A changeling of sorts
Attended first by Infant Esau
Then the Sirenoforms
Who jabber and squeal
Through breached sternums
Waving their dorsal flaps
Noisily sucking
I saw you spoon out the giblets
To Zoophagous Margie
Heard you coo ever so sweetly
Like an indulgent mommy
At her guttural chuckling
Then wipe clean the spittle
From her mouth and chin
I watched you there
Thriving
As if among your own
An hysteria gaining
With drink and time
So flushed with pleasure

At the fact of your presence
Your comeliness and bearing
How they primped
And what a fuss they made
Over your choker
Your jacket
Your hair
How you inflamed them
Till appetite crackled
Fat in the skillet
Clementine the Pigboy
Could not help but touch you
Your hips and arms
Your breasts
I turned away
And you said nothing
Emboldened, then Zep, Jo-Jo
And the Crocodile Girl too
Still you said nothing
And the noise
You had to have seen me
But for the din
Might have heard me
Call to you
Call out your name

Luminoso e dolce

Suzerainty

Impetigo

Colorless green ideas
    sleep furiously

Titrate

Spinners&darners

Farallons

Dag

Frottage

Slow loris

Gating

A bit of the other

Cuisse de nymphe

Chamfer

Amber, civet and musk cods

Wahoo McDaniel

Chlamydia

Mortised-and-tenoned

Huitzilopochtli

A bit of rough

Chalumeaux

Dingleberry

Esculent

Wing nut

Sforzato

Ten dwarfs took turns doing
    headstands
    on the carpet

Woonsocket

Lally-column

Gutta-percha

Galaxy Giveaway Girl

Coffered

Feminine intensive

Epicanthus

A cup of tea, a Bex and
    a good lie down

Lawyer Malloy

Stuka

Portage

Columbarium

Irwin Corey

Melisma

Fest und Locker

Korsakoff's Syndrome

Ocarina

Fatwa

Quoi d'autre

Guelph

Chopsaki

Hibiscus

Rhinoplasty

Ashes hauled

Dweeb

Good night, Mrs. Calabash

What the Science of the Ancients Told

The ancient Cathayans made of this one science an art,
which is in their reading of the human pulse.
Upon placing his finger on a certain wrist
the expert physician with nicety could tell
how fared each of the five vital organs
and the condition of the six viscera as well.

For they did this by means of comparison,
philosophy and science being one and the same.
A measure first was taken of the human vibration,
then set beside the cosmic ether, its vibration.
Next, consideration was given the time of year,
after that the patient's *dominant element,*

finally, the nature of his *vital force.*
The physician now brought forth his tables to consult:
the five *tsang* pulses, the six *fu* pulses,
the seven *pyan* pulses, the eight *li* pulses
and the nine *tau* pulses. Thus, he would perpend
certain natural objects, whether they be analogous:

a blade of small onion, solid within
       a stone bullet shot out of a crossbow
    a drop of water
              down   a drum-head
     a grate in a passage   a hole in a flute
a filament of hair   scattering leaves;

thereby, surmising whether the pulse be *creeping*
or *formicant, undulatory, thrilling* or *harsh*;
and if, say, *undulatory*, refining it further still
to *a fast-going she-camel whose girth slips through*
the unequal motion of the fore and hind feet.
Whereupon, having assayed its innate thingness,

the physician would then consider the pulse as action:
frisking fish   rolling thunder   a bird flying low
       branches of a willow tree in a gentle spring zephyr
            feathers agitated by the wind
       the pace of a toad embarrassed by weeds
drops of water dripping through a crack in the roof.

And, having explored the character of this pulse
first through its resemblance to things in nature,
then through its resemblance to actions in nature,
the physician, after no small period, considered at last
the nature of the pulse in relation to human action;
and he would evaluate carefully these six:

throwing earth over an object
going by stealth
the strokes of a knife point
a knife scraping bamboo
puffing and blowing in going upstairs
turning back

And thereby, the physician, who was also a sage,
might know, after checking first the tongue and eyes,
whether the affliction be dropsy or heartache,
what had gone inspissate or a putrefaction in the gorge.
But this is not the end of the science,
this science called Sphygmology, there is more.

For as there are human vibrations so too does Heaven
contract and dilate in manifold measures of its own.
And this not only the Cathayans knew
but the healer Avicenna, too, healer and philosopher
in the age of the Caliphate of 'Abbāsid.
And as Galen before him, so Avicenna described this pulse

in terms of rhythm, meters, one kind of pulse
even called *Kin* by the Chinese, *Tseng* as well,
which is a kind of zither with thirteen strings.
It is through music we are put in harmony with Heaven,
and this music consists of pulses, long and short,
with many changes of interval between, velocity too,

not to mention strength and all manner of degree.
Avicenna tells us, lays out in his famous *Canon*
which entails all of medicine, some philosophy also,
that if one knows the relations of loudness and softness,
their sequence and intervals, regular or not,
and knows these things as they abide in the pulse,

which has an order to itself much as Heaven does
in its perpetual breathings, almost a kind of song,
that would oftentimes seem far beyond our skills or ken
but of whose harmonies we yearn to partake,
well then, should one find the right succession of notes
great joy would follow, that along with matchless health.

The Dead Canary

Behold the dead canary on Saturn,
rain matting its feathers and runneling
past its vivid beak.
               —Someone's poisoning them,

the old lady says, then gives her black Scottie
a yank before he inhales the remains.
               —Sad, sad, sad,
the old lady says, head bowed

over the tiny yellow thing, so delicate
and gay, so exquisite in its proportions
and shape, collapsed there on the bleary pavement.

Then flashes me an eldritch look in passing.
As if I spent my days with a dropper,
skulking about in search of their feeders,

alive only to cancel out their color and song.
I would as soon hammer a butterfly
against a wood fence with a sixpenny nail

and go about with its powders on my sleeve
to savor under black light later that evening,
alone in my rooms with my stoppers and vials.

No, no, I am a clement soul, not a beast,
and fill with pity at its ruined wings,
but marvel as well at what a picture it makes,

nicely off-center and ravaged enough
but not too, spread out there
on a square of sidewalk—framed:

if only for an hour or a day
until a cat comes along to tear it apart
or it's sluiced to the gutter by rain.

On Top of the Hill: Montclair

The air is sweeter on top of the hill
with rhododendrons in bloom
near Eagle Rock, getting up toward the Watchungs,
homes as big as small-town city halls,
mock Tudor or porticoes like Monticello.
It seems like no one's in these homes at all

as a beat-up old sedan blows past
full of big kids screaming
                              —*Get off 'a the road, you* . . .

It's the start of Saturday night.
I wonder if the kids indoors can hear,
and if they'd like to be along, sucking beer

from quart bottles, headed to a party
with the bass cranked till the car throbs.
But those kids are a different kind,
and besides, they're gone, long passed
and silence is back now like a heavy arm
on top of the lid of evening.

The shadows at this hour compound, twine
and pass across one another on different planes.
It is a time of delicate melancholy
before the lamps inside are switched on

and the voices there inside come on
and then the ragged details surface

like a photo in its bath of chemicals.
Out the south windows and east-facing windows
a swath of meadowlands and old manufacturing
towns below, and farther south the lights
just coming on now with the dusk
of downtown Newark, and beyond,

at the horizon on clear nights,
the crests of Manhattan's tallest towers.
But not tonight, tonight the flats
sit under an earthen-yellow haze, steeping.
Down there, under the floodlights
a few low-rent ballgames are gearing up, the players

stretching, shagging flies. The stands
begin to fill, the men flushed and noisy, a heat
picked up at the local bodega,
and the wives dolled up like Nefertiti.
While up here on the hill beside the park
it is lovely, utterly still,

the fragrance of magnolia delicately restrained
in the cool of the hour before dark.

Someone Named Gutierrez:

A Dream, A Western

Outside the cantina
with you in the backseat of a ruined DeSoto,
torn upholstery, vinyl mange
and the big old radio's static frying
what could only be a Dixie Cups tune.
Things had gone terribly bad,
and Slim, who drove us the whole long way
through chaparral and dust,
was in there now, with them,
asking for the money he had no right to,
had no right to even ten years back
when the fire was, or so he says.
They nearly killed him then,
the fool, the braggart, the Suicide Kid,
just itching after a good old-timey
late afternoon cowboy send-off,
blood and gold and glinting side arms,

with us stuck back there yet, hove-to
in the backseat like two kids
waiting for Dad.
                When you touched me,
the lightest of touches, the most unforeseen,
carelessly along the wrist.
I nearly came unglued.
I mean, I knew about Ramon,

that lovely boy—and for so long,
the two of you. I cherish that photo still,
your white tam-o'-shanter, his red TransAm.
Then I became water.
Then, from what had once been my chest,
a plant made of light effloresced.
Thus, our adventure began, our slow-motion
free fall through the vapors and oils.
I stammered at your white flesh.

                        And that,
that's when the shooting began.

Under the floorboards Shadow and Smoke bark
through these windy summer nights, always
at queer intervals. Something's got up their noses
or call and response with a distant yard.
All summer long awakened from dreams by barks,
remembering each of them through, shabby kinescopes.
The guys upstairs come fetch them in the morning
and disappear till night, always leaving
the light on in the storeroom,
to make it more cheerful, I suppose.
Perhaps even the radio on low, tuned
to the easy-listening channel, *KBLX, The Quiet Storm,*
102.9 F.M.
            I've grown used to them down there,
like the sound of the streetcar right before dawn
with its keening whine and groan.
But the renters promise to be out by fall.

I thought of you the other night,
walking in the hills late, later than usual,
the moon only a day or two from full.
How it was full the night you arrived,
which is something you seem to plan, saying:
—Next full moon I'll be in Torres Strait,
P.O. Box Thursday Island.

I've been meaning to write.
The rest of the *naked ladies* finally came up,
dozens of them, waving their pink heads in the fog.
Only the one, poking through the dirt when you left,
is a stalk now with a shriveled head.
They do look garish so late in the summer,
like Rockettes in a dusty frontier town.

But you see, none of it really fits quite right,
the pieces I find or that come round, unbidden.
I had wanted badly to get in that part,
the *wog from the western suburbs*,
your momma's fluttering hands and the trip in
with Grandma on Sunday, the two hours by train
and tram all the way to over near Bondi
for black bread and smelly salami . . .

The bits we choose to keep and what leave out—
these absences take on a life themselves.

Toys

The janitor washing the blackboard
in Mrs. Turnaud's class

February night not too far
from the border with Vermont

snowless, and still a little stoned

thinks he caught a patch
of aurora borealis out the window

or maybe just a headlight off a cloud

———

Thank you for kissing me just then
It was getting to be rather a swarm in there
with the tendrils, suckers and shoots

no purpose, no end in sight

syntax a lost dynasty

———

That child is in terror
terror of himself

You can tell by his face
how it's wrong in three parts

and with a helmet of busy bruised air
framing it

the parents, insensible
walk chattering behind

He's going to hurt himself
He's going to hurt himself, soon

———

Look at the colored liquids and string beans
in a jar, pickled

the carved mahogany sideboard

so old and so dark, like Europe

———

The gaunt timpanist
with the visiting symphony orchestra

sits by himself on a concrete bench
in the abandoned pedestrian mall

Sunday with dead oak and maple
leaves skittering past

in this lovely provincial city
renowned for its love

of the arts

———

She's a drunkard but still pretty
40-ish, oddly athletic

The sidewalk might as well be
the top of a sawhorse
she walks so daintily with her pint
in a small brown bag

when suddenly a terrific boom
ripples across the sky overhead
brilliant afternoon

It's the celebrated Blue Angels
rocketing east to west
in their Tomcat fighters

nearly on top of each other
tight diamond formation

their contrails feathering behind
come apart and vanish into sky

———

The hobbyist in his room, alone
under the blue turret

his work of many years now done

each row of matchsticks flawlessly
joined, canted, plumb

the fading smell of epoxy

The Conversation

This then was the conversation
There were others, of course, not a few
But there was this one
Time and again
The one that truly mattered
And the others, well
I can barely remember the others
But this one
That drove all ahead of it
A great wave or wind
That tore apart the very ground
That sent up a wall of debris
That would leave nothing
Could leave only nothing
By design
If asked
If one could ask a brute thing
Inquire of rock or bone
Entreat
Put one's own arm
One's hand
Down into the engine of its force
To know its workings
Even if torn to pieces
To have felt down there
Felt something
Move

An intelligence of parts
Gear and ratchet
Anything
But not this
No, not this, ever, no
Only the fact of it
This whirlwind
Why not
A biblical reek to it
Perfect
But scaled down
Way down
And kept in the vestibule
An ornament
A kinetic sculpture
In the corner
On a stand
An *objet d'art*

Before Dawn on Bluff Road

The crow's raw hectoring cry
scoops clean an oval divot
of sky, its fading echo
among the oaks and poplars swallowed
first by a jet banking west
then the Erie-Lackawanna
sounding its horn as it comes through the tunnel
through the cliffs to the river
and around the bend of King's Cove Bluff,
full of timber, Ford chassis, rock salt.

You can hear it in the dark
from beyond what was once the amusement park.
And the wind carries along as well,
from down by the river,
when the tide's just so,
the drainage just so,
the chemical ghost of old factories,
the rotted piers and warehouses:
lye, pigfat, copra from Lever Bros.,
formaldehyde from the coffee plant,

dyes, unimaginable solvents—
a soup of polymers, oxides,
tailings fifty years old
seeping through the mud, the aroma
almost comforting by now, like food,

wafting into my childhood room
with its fevers and dreams.
My old parents asleep,
only a few yards across the hall,
door open—lest I cry?
                    I remember
almost nothing of my life.

Diablo: *A Recipe*

(For W. S. Di Piero)

Caro mio, the hot must dwell among the dark
the orange habanero

burning like a candle in a terra-cotta jar
and the onion tuned, just so

that when the mud commences to bubble, to streak
and to spit, a barely audible sweetness

is there too; but still, still
that torrid little fist commands

the temperate hand, the wooden spoon, the meats
nothing will avail

but patience, as in many things
in love, say, or with a poem

but in this the most of all
for as the first of afternoon's late shadows falls

and as I-95's muffled rumbling
ebbs and flows in the distance, crossing the river

beyond the big beech tree, its leaves flaring gold
only now, after how many hours

the meat and marrow slip from the bone
the dark pasilla and chorizo show

as currents in a muddy river show
only a shade or two off

but careful not to turn the lights on
or all of it is lost

for the broth and the room are now as one
one fabric of shadow

broken only by the blue flame of the burner
turned very low

and so, the moment has come
for the first, the most important glass of wine

a big red, why not a Merlot
because only now, alone in this room

dark and quiet as a chapel
the garlic has slowly begun to bloom

and the wine in the back of your throat
will be made sonorous by it

then it is time, after much stirring
and some contemplation

to find the appropriate tune
perhaps one of Schubert's final sonatas

and take up your spoon once more
and for the first time taste

how the ferocious one, the brute
because of the lily has been seduced

and burns still, indelibly
but like the small blue flame in the darkened room

Red pear leaves take the light at four,
and a patch of brick on the south, rear wall
stripped of wisteria: the two reds embering
a little while then dying back into the shadows.
A corner of the afternoon is all,
maybe half an hour, not much more—
October, November . . . the beech tree bare now.

Sunday's blow would have done it.
And always the Interstate out there, like surf,
running up to Boston or south to New York.
And broken-up city across the river,
a used-to-be textile port, gutted.
One good high-rise, an old-style stepback,
and the power plant on Point Street,

glowing orange now in sodium light,
highlines feeding out of it, dripping
with porcelain isolators. We watch it every night,
red lights blinking from the three tall stacks,
the staggered sequence of its flashing crowns
scaring off the geese and Cessnas.
The turbines and generators roar, never ceasing.

We went inside. We saw it. We heard.
He made us lean underneath and see the flame
through the thick glass, deep in the steel.

And then we went back into the wind,
past the Nightingale Metals truck
and across the bridge on foot. No one saw.
No one knows. The eyes of the beech.

We have examined these afternoons
like a slide taken from a petri dish,
spindles of living matter, degraded, fraying,
taking on new shapes, gray, opalescent.
The red lights in the distance, blinking.
The roar in the boiler house.
The drawn shades.

Self-portrait

It was a *lost* dream, a bridges and heights
and headed home dream, but too long,
far too long and mazy and all the wrong tone.
And then there was that station, so massive,
with its tiers, platforms, girders and steps,
trains rushing through on the express track,
filled to bursting, commuters illuminated,
each face vivid, highlighted—is that you?—
exasperation, fatigue, concern at the time.
But the time was all wrong; it was late,
way late, the station ready to close.
The subways never close, you say, even in dreams:
empty, only rarely if ever a train, but open.
This was no ordinary station, or dream.

You could see Manhattan in the far distance,
big towers beyond the raggedy miles
of tenements, viaducts, frozen playgrounds.
Like the view from the Nor'easter headed south
as it winds its way around the Bronx,
right before it dips down into the tunnel.
But this place would have had to be in Queens.
At the start it was a plane I was headed for,
headed for that morning from quite another town.
This must be the old *train to the plane*,
the one that lets you off way out by Kennedy.
But that got shut down years ago.

Now I was far from anything, Jersey especially.
I always head back to Jersey in a pinch.

My two suitcases were gone as well, both black,
one large, one small. My shoes too, also black.
There I was, lost, weaving left and right,
pitiful as a bug caught out in the light.
Way down there in the bowels with the gated-up
shoe-shine, burger and newsstands, a cop, a drunk.
But a barbershop of sorts still open and lit
and oddly partitioned into three distinct rooms:
one with a man fitting rubber skin skulls
onto mannequin heads; the next a barber
fussily attending to three bald heads;
the next what could only be a tiny morgue,
but with those very same heads from the barber's,
only this time like death masks of Renaissance popes.

That's when I ran onto this burly black guy,
security or some kind of station chief.
He was short with me for being there but nice enough
and led me on a search for my two bags.
Through horrible rooms: bodies, gunnysacks,
leavings from some old and gruesome jumble sale.
—*The two last rooms on earth*, I heard myself say.
And still no bags, but when I looked down
there were my shoes, back on my feet again,

except each from a different pair. Odd, that,
but I was plenty glad to have them on,
stuck by myself in the middle of nowhere
with the station shutting down for the night
and who knows what waiting out there in the shadows.

Somehow it had gotten to be dawn.
I found myself standing up to my ankles in weeds
with rusted fenders and a torn-down fence.
Manhattan sticking up in the filmy distance.
Lots of birds, planes too, out of Kennedy.
When two ugly-looking kids were headed my way.
Didn't like how this was shaping up at all.
If I had to bolt, the weeds would hold me back.
But they turned out to be sweet, bewildered boys,
in wonderment at my simply standing there.
I believe I had on a flannel shirt, a plaid,
sun igniting the wet, dark smells of earth.
It was all so eerily gentle and strange
I might as well have been Captain Cook in the Marquesas.

Printed in the USA
CPSIA information can be obtained
at www.ICGtesting.com
LVHW091147150724
785511LV00005B/605

9 780374 525842